華藝 III

Oriental Flower Arrangement III

Im Wha Kong

華藝 Ⅲ

Oriental Flower Arrangement Ⅲ

任 華公 著　Im Wha Kong

All rights reserved throughout the world.
No part of this book may be reproduced in any form
without permission in writing from the publisher.

© Copyright in Japan 1990 by Im Wha Kong
Photographs by Shufunotomo Co., Ltd.

First printing, 1990

Published by Shufunotomo Co., Ltd.
2-9, Kanda Surugadai, Chiyoda-ku, Tokyo 101, Japan

Wha Kong Hoe Corporation;
(Im, Wha Kong Flower Arrangement Society)
10, Tongui-dong, Jongro-ku, Seoul, Korea
Tel: (Seoul) (02) 737-6305

Printed in Japan
ISBN: 4-07-974328-9

華藝Ⅲ
1990年4月＊第1刷發行

著者＊任華公
寫眞＊宇垣健次
編輯＊木下庚子
　　　西邑桃代
取材協力＊大韓民國文化公報部
　　　　　梨花女子大學校家政科學大學
發行者＊石川晴彦
發行處＊主婦の友社
　　　　〒101 日本國東京都千代田區神田駿河台2－9
　　　　電話　東京(03)294－1118
社團法人華公會＊〒110－040
　　　　　大韓民國서울特別市鍾路區通義洞10
　　　　　電話　서울(02)737－6305

Contents

目　次

Preface

To my friends, the lovers of flowers throughout the world:

Ten years have passed since my book, *Oriental Flower Arrangement I* was first published. During that time a sequel, *Oriental Flower Arrangement II*, was also published, and both of these books have been reprinted several times. I now take great pleasure in introducing you to the third in the series, *Oriental Flower Arrangement III*.

In many countries around the world, the warm reception given *Oriental Flower Arrangement I* and *II* have helped to deepen and strengthen my ties with flower-loving friends.

In *Oriental Flower Arrangement III*, I have used varieties of flowers and vases that originated in many different countries to create the arrangements. I wrote this book with a spirit of humility and the aim of revealing the beauty of nature and value of life through flower arrangement.

I would like to express my heartfelt gratitude and appreciation to all of the staff of the Office of Cultural Information of the Republic of Korea and to Shufunotomo Co., Ltd. for the kind understanding and cooperation they have extended to me for the publication of this book.

I sincerely hope that readers will keep this book close at hand, so that they can easily refer to it or enjoy reading it casually, and in some small way, enhance the quality of their lives.

Im Wha Kong

前　文

世界의 꽃친구들에게

　華藝 I 이 出版된 지 十年이 되었습니다. 그 동안에 華藝 II 가 나오고 각기 冊들은 版을 거듭하여 華藝 III 을 내게 되어 기쁩니다.

　여러 나라에서 많은 機會에 華藝 I 과 華藝 II 는 더 한층 나와 꽃친구들을 따뜻하게 맺어 주었습니다.

　그리고 이 冊에서는 널리 여러 나라의 꽃과 花器를 作品에 썼습니다.

　꽃을 通하여 自然의 아름다움과 生命의 존엄함을 되새기면서 謙虛한 마음으로 이 冊을 엮었습니다.

　出版에 이르기까지 文化公報部와 主婦의 友社의 理解있는 協助에 深深한 感謝의 뜻을 表합니다.

　東洋의 꽃을 사랑하는 世界의 꽃친구들이 가벼운 마음으로 즐겁게 옆에 놓을 수 있는, 그리고 生活의 質을 向上시키는 데 도움이 되는 冊이 되기를 바라마지 않습니다.

Oriental Flower Arrangement

One thing most Asian people have in common is a true love of nature. This love of nature has strongly influenced the cultures that have arisen over the centuries. Oriental flower arrangement is no exception; its most important rule is to respect the essential nature and characteristics of plants.

By "essential nature of plants," I mean such natural properties as the tendency of plants to grow towards light and to extend branches and leaves, to conform to the needs of their environment. By "characteristics," I mean the unique characteristics of every species of plants.

Pine trees have their unique characteristics, while viny plants have their viny characteristics. For example, the characteristic of the clematis vine is its tendency to droop unless it is supported by something around which it can twine. However, even if there is no support, clematis will naturally grow towards the sky. This is the essential nature of clematis. We should regard every plant as a living creature, with vitality and a will to grow.

In arranging clematis, our knowledge of the essential nature and characteristics of the plant leads us to direct the tip of the vine upward, as if it were growing. We do not do this in conformance to a prescribed rule; flower arrangers have naturally developed this technique in an attempt to express the natural beauty of flowers by revealing their essential nature and characteristics.

Flower arrangers show their true appreciation of nature by scrupulously attending to the treatment of every branch, every flower and every leaf until they are satisfied with their work. One can see that an arrangement also reflects the personality and feelings of the flower arrangers. Whether one's days are quiet or hectic, the arranger's state of mind is clearly reflected in a floral composition.

An individual flower arrangement is the product of the arranger's unfettered ideas and interpretations of the characteristic beauty and properties of the materials and container. Through flower arrangement, the arranger's entire personality is revealed.

As our lives and living environments have changed, the role of flowers in our lives has also changed dramatically. Today we not only arrange flowers to decorate our home, but also for ourselves, for guests, for various private and public occasions and even for store displays and exhibitions. We can now see flower arrangements in variety of forms in virtually every part of the world.

In arranging flowers, we must maintain an awareness of our changing surroundings and lifestyles, the increasing diversity of available materials, and most importantly, the attitudes of our contemporaries. Rational thinking and knowledge are of course important for people today, but we shouldn't place too much emphasis on them, or we may cheapen our value system. The result would be apathy or the negation of humane feelings.

We must keep our minds open and fresh, and be ready to accept whatever can stimulate our thinking. Often, the most impressive flower arrangements are those which were created with an open, natural frame of mind.

Let us sharpen our senses to enable us to appreciate the real beauty we observe with our eyes, to discriminate what is beautiful from what is not and to arange flowers with a joyous feeling of natural appreciation.

華 藝

東洋사람들은 끝없이 自然을 사랑해 왔습니다.

그리고 自然에 對한 사랑은 오랫동안 여러가지 文化를 가꾸게 하였습니다.

自然을 사랑하는 마음은 꽃을 꽂는 데 있어 草木의 自然出生을 무엇보다 소중하게 생각합니다.

草木의 自然이란 草木에 共通하는 性質, 즉 빛을 向해 가지나 잎이 뻗어가고 環境에 따라 生育하는 모양입니다.

出生이란 草木마다에 있는 固有한 性狀입니다.

소나무는 소나무같이 덩굴은 덩굴답게 자라고 있습니다.

크리마치스의 덩굴은 감겨 갈 것이 없으면 늘어져 버립니다. 이것은 自然스러운 모양입니다. 그러나 크리마치스는 감겨서 올라 갈것이 없을 때에도 다시 위로 向해 뻗어 나가려고 합니다.

이것이 크리마치스의 出生의 모양새입니다.

이것은 草木의 自然의 모양새 안에 있는 살아가려는 힘을 감싸고 있는 意思를 볼 수 있습니다.

크리마치스를 꽂을 때 그 出生을 알고 있기에 늘어진 가지끝을 위로 向하도록 하여 生氣있게 표현할 수 있는 것입니다.

그것은 늘어진 가지 끝을 위로 向하게 꽂으라는 법을 만드는 것이 아니라 自然을 사랑하고 自然을 즐기는 사람들이 꽃을 꽂을 때 저절로 自然의 出生을 깨닫고 그들의 아름다움을 찾아내는 方法으로 쓰여지는 技法이 되는 것입니다.

그리고 더 아름답게 더 한층 自己 마음을 表現하고자 한 줄기 가지에도 한 잎의 잎새에도 마음을 써서 線을 고르고 가지를 정리해 나갑니다.

꽃을 꽂는 데 있어 꽂는 사람의 人品과 마음씨는 作品에 그대로 反映되게 마련입니다.

조용하게 마음이 가라앉아 있을 때, 쫓기듯이 바쁠 때 등 그때 그때 꽂아지는 作品은 그대로 나타나게 됩니다.

作者의 自由로운 發想아래 草木에 의해 創作되는 個性的인 作品은 素材나 花器들의 固有한 아름다움 혹은 각기 다른 모양새의 構成으로 인해 이루어집니다.
그리고 작품은 作者의 全人格을 드러내는 자리이기도 합니다.

꽃을 꽂는 環境은 時代나 地域, 또는 住居環境의 變化, 나아가서 素材의 多樣化 등으로 인해 항상 流動的입니다. 그러나 가장 重要한 것은 그 時代를 사는 사람들의 '생각'이라 여겨집니다.

合理的인 分別과 知識이 社會生活을 하는 사람들에게 있어 必要한 것이기는 하지만 이것에 치우치다보면 때로는 環境의 影響을 받아 價値觀이 바뀌어 마음을 설레이는 感動하는 마음마저 무디게 되는 것이 아닐까 생각도 됩니다.

新鮮한 印象을 순수히 받아들이는 마음은 비어놓은 마음에 있지 아니한가 합니다.

그저 自然스럽게 꽂은 꽃이 사람들의 마음에 파고드는 것을 우리들은 가끔 볼 수가 있습니다.

自己自身의 눈으로 본 그리고 느낀, 아름다운 感動을 날카로운 감각으로 대담하게 판단하여 따뜻한 사랑의 마음으로 가꾸면서 즐겁게 꽃을 꽂아가고 싶습니다.

Creative Works
Arranged in Vases
of the World

自然의 꽃
世界의 花器에

Materials: Pine, cattleya and aged tree
Container: White porcelain vase

素材　소나무, 洋蘭, 古木
花器　白磁花瓶

Materials: Plum, tree peony and orchid leaves
Container: White porcelain basin

素材 梅花, 牡丹, 蘭잎
花器 白磁水盤

Materials: Pine, moth orchid, narcissus, Buddha's hand orange and aged tree
Container: White porcelain basin

素材 소나무, 洋蘭, 水仙花, 佛手柑, 古木
花器 白磁水盤

Materials: Nandina, pine and cattleya
Container: White porcelain basin

素材　南天，소나무，洋蘭
花器　白磁花器

Materials: Pine, narcissus and greenbrier
Container: Kaisser Flower vase

素材　소나무, 水仙花, 山歸來
花器　카이자花器

Materials: Sweet pea and blue star
Container: Original glass vase by Hotoku Masuda

素材　스위트피-, 부루-스타-
花器　手製유리花器(益田芳德作)

Materials: Sweet pea and asparagus myriocladus
Container: Flower vase by Johan van Loon

素材　스위트피－, 미리오그라타스아스파라거스
花器　로－젠탈－花器

Materials: Yulan, weeping forsythia, azalea and aged tree
Container: White porcelain wine bottle

素材　木蓮，山茱萸，아제리아，古木
花器　白磁酒瓶

Materials: Japanese quince, rape flower, root of greenbrier and aged tree
Container: White porcelain octagonal vase

素材　山檀花, 유채화, 山歸來뿌리, 古木
花器　白磁八角花瓶

Materials: Freesia and ranunculus
Container: Iwata glass water basin

素材　후리ー지아，라낭큐러스
花器　유리花器(岩田)

Material: Poppy
Container: Iwata glass vase

素材　양귀비꽃
花器　유리花器(岩田)

Material: Poppy
Container: Flower vase by B. Winblad

素材　양귀비꽃
花器　로－젠탈－花瓶

19

Material: Azalea and aged tree
Container: White porcelain vase

素材　映山紅，古木
花器　白磁水盤

Materials: Azalea and aged tree
Container: White porcelain vase

素材　映山紅，古木
花器　白磁花瓶

Materials: Rose and blue star
Container: Iwata glass vase

素材　薔薇, 부루-스타-
花器　유리花器(岩田)

Materials: Rose, New
Zealand flax, ivy
and false spirea
Container: White porcelain
water basin

素材　薔薇, 뉴－사이랑,
　　　沈至梅, 담장이덩굴
花器　白磁水盤

Materials: Rose and lace
flower
Container: French vase

素材　薔薇, 레－스홀라워－
花器　佛蘭西製花瓶

23

Materials: Lily magnolia and orchid
Container: White porcelain octagonal vase

素材　木蓮，洋蘭
花器　白磁八角花瓶

Materials: Lily magnolia, cattleya, tree peony and aged tree
Container: White porcelain water basin

素材　木蓮，洋蘭，牡丹，古木
花器　白磁水盤

Materials: Sweet flag, azalea and poet's jasmine
Container: White porcelain water basin

素材　菖蒲，철쭉，素馨
花器　白磁水盤

Materials: Sweet flag, Japanese snow flower, white enkianthus, maple and aged tree
Container: Large white porcelain bowl

素材　菖浦，빈도리，철쭉，등대꽃，단풍나무，古木
花器　白磁大鉢

Materials: Japanese dogwood, day lily and aged tree
Container: Flower vase by Akira Yoshida

素材　산딸나무, 감초, 古木
花器　粉青花器

Materials: Yellow lily, mountain ash and moss-covered azalea branch
Container: White porcelain vase

素材　黄百合，마가목，古木
花器　白磁花器

Materials: Hydrangea, maple, greenbrier and aged tree
Container: White porcelain water basin

素材　수국, 단풍나무, 山歸來, 古木
花器　白磁水盤

Materials: Hydrangea, Japanese bulrush, gardenia, bleached vine of kiwifruits and
lace flower
Container: White porcelain bowl

素材　수국, 용수초, 치자꽃, 표백다래덩굴, 레ー스꽃
花器　白磁鉢

Materials: Nasturtium and bleached vine of kiwifruits
Container: Flower vase by Martin Freyer

素材　金蓮花, 표백다래덩굴
花器　로－젠탈－花瓶

Material: Begonia (Rose Pearl)
Container: Flower vase by Johan van Loon

素材　베고니아
花器　로－젠탈－花瓶

Materials: Tulip and spirea
thumbergii
Container: Glass vase

素材　튜울립, 물싸리꽃
花器　유리花器

Materials: Anthurium, orchid and asparagus smilax
Container: White porcelain vase with narrow neck

素材　앤스룸ー，洋蘭，스마일락스
花器　白磁酒瓶

Materials: Allium giganteum, marguerite
and Solomon's seal leaves
Container: White porcelain container

素材　아륨ー，마ー가렛，둥굴레잎
花器　白磁鉢

Materials: Anthurium and asparagus
myriocladus
Container: White porcelain bowl

素材　앤스룜ー，미리오그라타스아스파라거스
花器　白磁筆筒

Materials: Plantain lily and false
            spirea
Container: White porcelain water
            basin

素材　玉簪花，沈至梅
花器　白磁水盤

Material: Lily of the valley
Container: White porcelain vase

素材　비비취꽃
花器　白磁花器

Material: Plantain lily
Container: White porcelain bowl

素材　玉簪花
花器　白磁花器

Materials: Azalea, maple, lily and aged tree
Container: Silla earthenware vase

素材　철쭉, 단풍나무, 百合, 古木
花器　新羅土器

Materials: Nandina, orchids and aged tree
Container: Silla earthenware vase

素材　南天，洋蘭，古木
花器　新羅土器

Materials: Fiveleaf akebia and orchid
Container: Yu dynasty earthenware bottle

素材 으름, 洋蘭
花器 李朝白磁

Materials: Clematis, oncidium and alocasia
Container: White porcelain vase

素材　크리마티스，洋蘭，아로카시아
花器　白磁花瓶

Materials: Japanese rose and greenbrier
Container: Silla earthenware vase

素材　薔薇，山歸來
花器　新羅土器

Materials: Orchids and aged tree
Container: White porcelain bowl

素材　洋蘭，古木
花器　白磁大鉢

Materials: Waxflower and golden calla
Container: Blue glass bowl

素材　왁스홀라워-, 노란카-라릴리-
花器　남色유리볼

Materials: Carnation and sweet bouvardia
Container: Blue glass pitcher

素材　카네이션, 스위-트부바리듸아
花器　남色유리핏챠-

44

Materials: Carnation and sweet bouvardia
Container: Blue glass bowl

素材 카네이션, 스위－트부바리듸아
花器 남色유리볼

Materials: Sunflower, Japanese bulrush and
caradium
Container: Flower vase by Tapio Wirkkala

素材　해바라기꽃,　龍鬚草,　카라듐－
花器　로－젠탈－花器

Materials: Swertia japonica Makino and
Lycoris radiata Herb.
Container: Glass container

素材　쓴풀,　리고리스
花器　유리花器

Materials: Lycoris and hydrangea
Container: Kosta Boda glass vase

素材　리고리스，나무수국
花器　스웨－덴製유리花器

Materials: Hydrangea and oncidium
Container: Italian vase

素材　나무수국，洋蘭
花器　이태리製花瓶

Materials: Fiveleaf akebia, orchid and aged tree
Container: French bowl

素材　으름，洋蘭，古木
花器　불란서製鉢

Material: Cyclamen
Container: White porcelain water basin

素材　시크라멘
花器　白磁花器

Material: Lotus
Container: White porcelain water basin

素材　蓮꽃
花器　白磁水盤

Materials: Cattleya, oncidium and adiantum
Container: White porcelain octagonal vase

素材　洋蘭，아지안담
花器　白磁八角花瓶

Materials: Pine and moth orchid
Container: White porcelain water basin

素材　소나무, 洋蘭
花器　白磁花器

Materials: Fiveleaf akebia and cuttleya
Container: Flower vase by Claus Josef Riedel

素材　으름, 洋蘭
花器　로-젠탈-花器

Materials: Hydrangea, prairie gentian,
            sweet scabiosa and Chinese
            miscanthus
Container: White porcelain bowl

素材　나무수국, 크리마티스, 스카비오사, 억새
花器　白磁鉢

Materials: Clematis, zebra grass and aged
            tree
Container: White porcelain bowl

素材　크리마티스, 얼룩억새, 古木
花器　白磁鉢

Materials: Pampas grass, ear of great cat's tail, monstera and groriosa
Container: White porcelain bowl

素材　팜파스그라스，부들，몬스텔라，글로리오사
花器　白磁鉢

Materials: Sunflower, great burnet, fiveleaf akebia, beard grass and aged tree
Container: White porcelain vase

素材　해바라기꽃, 오디풀, 으름, 베어드그라스, 古木
花器　白磁筆筒

Materials: Mountain ash, gentian and great burnet
Container: White porcelain water basin

素材　마가목, 용담, 오디풀
花器　白磁水盤

Materials: Japanese quince, narcissus and azalea
Container: White porcelain water basin

素材　山檀花，水仙花，아젤리아
花器　白磁水盤

Materials: Carnation and chloranthus
          glaber
Container: White porcelain vase

素材　카네이션, 죽절초
花器　白磁花器

Materials: Rose hips, akebia and groriosa
Container: White porcelain bowl

素材　薔薇열매, 글로리오사, 으름
花器　白磁鉢

Materials: Rose, rose hips and aged
        tree
Container: White porcelain water
        basin

素材　薔薇꽃, 薔薇열매, 古木
花器　白磁水盤

Materials: Bittersweet and dahlia
Container: White porcelain bottle

素材　까치밥덩굴, 다알리아꽃
花器　白磁호로瓶

Materials: Japanese winterberry, gentian, anemone hupehensis L. and aged tree
Container: White porcelain bowl

素材　落霜紅, 용담, 秋明菊, 古木
花器　白磁鉢

Materials: Sandersonia and hyacinth
Container: Small glass bottles

素材　산다－소니아，히야신스
花器　유리小瓶，黑白二個

Materials: Daffodil and asparagus smilax
Container: German crystal bowl

素材　데포딜-, 스마일락스
花器　독일제크리스탈볼-

Materials: Daffodil and marguerite
Container: British crystal bowl

素材　데포딜-, 마-가렛
花器　英國製크리스탈鉢

Materials: Camellia and greenbrier
Container: Italian glass container

素材　冬栢, 山歸來
花器　이태리製 유리鉢

Materials: Pomegranate, chrysanthemum, tinted azalea, Japanese winter berry and
　　　　　　aged tree
Container: White porcelain octagonal vase

素材　石榴, 菊花, 단풍든 철쭉, 落霜紅, 古木
花器　白磁八角瓶

Materials: Bleached weeping mulberry, camellia, paulownia pods and juniper
Container: White porcelain vase

素材　표백뽕나무, 冬栢, 梧桐꽃몽오리, 古木
花器　白磁花瓶

Materials: Mimosa acacia, anemone and tara vine
Container: White porcelain container

素材　미모사아카시아, 아네모네, 다래덩굴
花器　白磁鉢

Korean
Arrangements

環境의 꽃

Materials: Lotus seed, green brier, patrinia
　　　　 and small chrysanthemum
Container: White porcelain vase

素材　蓮밥, 山歸來, 마타리, 菊花
花器　白磁花瓶

Popchu Temple,
Stome Carved Relief Image
Ma-ae bul, Koryo era

俗離山 法住寺 磨崖如來倚像

Materials: Rose mallow and greenbrier

素材　부용꽃, 山歸來
花器　白磁水盤

Popchu Temple,
Stone Water Cistern (Lotus bud
stone cistern), 8th century
俗離山　法住寺　石蓮池

Materials: Rose of sharon and bittersweet
Container: White porcelain basin

素材 무궁화, 까치밥덩굴
花器 白磁花器

Popchu Temple
Background: Five-Storied Pagoda,
Palsan-jon, reconstructed 1624

俗離山 法住寺

Materials: Wild azalea, tara vine and
                 root of greenbrier
Container: White porcelain vase

素材　진달래, 다래덩굴, 山歸來뿌리
花器　白磁花瓶

Sorak Mountain, Rodge in
Hangyeryoung Pass
雪嶽山 寒溪嶺

Materials: Rose, Chinese lantern, greenbrier and red vine
Container: White porcelain basin

素材　薔薇，파리，山歸來，오동추
花器　白磁花器

The Site of Won-Gudan in Seoul
서울 圓丘檀

Materials: Pomegranate, zinnia elegans, greenbrier and tara vine
Container: White porcelain basin

素材　石榴，百日紅，山歸來，다래덩굴
花器　白磁水盤

Won-Gudan in Seoul
서울 圓丘壇

Materials: Pine, orchid, pomegranate
and driftwood
Container: White porcelain vase

素材　소나무, 洋蘭, 石榴, 古木
花器　白磁花瓶

Ewha Womens University,
Ah-Ryoung-Dang
서울 梨花女子大學 家政大學 關英堂

Materials: Pine, rose and tara vine
Container: White porcelain bowl

素材　소나무, 薔薇, 다래덩굴
花器　白磁鉢

Ewha Womens University, Ah-Ryoung-Dang
梨花女子大學校 家政大學 關英堂

Materials: Rose, gentian, bittersweet, fruit
         of Japanese quince, wild grape
         vine and aged tree
Container: Large white porcelain bowl

素材 薔薇, 용담, 까치밥, 山檀花열매,
     머루덩굴, 古木
花器 白磁大鉢

Ewha Womens University, Ah-Ryoung-Dang
     梨花女子大學校 家政大學 闕英堂

Materials: Rose, greenbrier, tara vine and aged tree
Container: Large white porcelain basin

素材　薔薇，山歸來，古木，다래덩굴
花器　白磁大水盤

Ewha Womens University, Ah-Ryoung-Dang
梨花女子大學校 家政大學 闆英堂

Techniques

꽃이야기

Cross Design　交　叉

When rose stems cross each other in an arrangement, they present a feeling of strength.

The overlapping, fluid lines of beard grass shown on the opposite page make a delicate impression, like the eyes of the mythical Chinese phoenix.

When masses of small white flowers such as baby's breath overlap, they create a sense of tremendous volume.

We must remember that the use of two non-parallel lines which don't actually meet makes a very different impression from that produced by two lines that intersect.

장미꽃 줄기는 直線의 交叉로 인해 한층 强한 表現을 할 수 있다.

蘭잎의 섬세하고 부드러운 曲線이 겹쳐져서 이루어지는 交叉에서 優雅한 鳳眼의 아름다움을 볼 수 있다.

또 베이비브레스같은 하얀 點의 무리가 交叉되었을 때는 그 空間構成에 따라 더한층 화려하게도 되고, 때로 量感을 나타낼 수가 있다.

線의 交叉에 있어 가지가 서로 닿았을 때와 떨어져 있을 때는 아주 다른 느낌을 준다.

Materials: Rose and bouvardia
Container: Flower vase by B. Winblad
素材　薔薇, 부바리디아
花器　로-젠탈-花瓶

Opposite page
Materials: Nerine, baby's breath and beard grass
Container: White porcelain bowl
素材　네리네, 베이비브레스, 베아드그라스
花器　白磁鉢

False Face   虛面이야기

The empty space enclosed within intersecting lines is called a "false face."

Depending on the lines which enclose it, the "false face" may appear flat or curved in different ways.

When considering the lines of your arrangements discriminate between straight lines, gently curving lines and strongly curving lines. You can add interest and vary arrangements by including both finely composed elements and roughly arranged elements.

Although the "false face" is blank, it acts as a plane, influencing the overall structure of floral compositions.

線과 線이 이어졌을 때에 이루는 空間의 面을 虛面이라고 한다.

虛面은 쓰여지는 線의 構成에 따라 平面으로 또는 曲面으로도 多樣하게 나타난다.

線은 直線, 느리게 휘어진 曲線, 움직임이 있는 빠른 曲線 등이 있고 또 굵기에도 변화가 많으므로 이를 잘 보고 虛面 構成에 變化를 주도록 한다.

虛面은 비어 있으면서 面의 役割을 다하고 作品의 構成에 있어 큰 影響을 끼친다.

Materials: Marguerite, barely and red vine
Container: Italian container with a handle
素材 마-가렛, 보리, 오동추
花器 이태리製손잡이花器

Opposite page (top)
Materials: Rose, thistle, red vine and
                    stauntonia
Container: White porcelain bowl
素材 薔薇, 엉겅퀴, 오동추, 으름
花器 白磁鉢

Opposite page (bottom)
Materials: Iris, marigold and red vine
Container: White porcelain water basin
素材 아이리스, 금잔화, 다래덩굴
花器 白磁花器

Flat-Style Flower Arrangement 平面型꽃

When arranging flowers in the flat style, flowers must be placed at varying distances from each other and must be of varying heights. A feeling of stability can be created by arranging taller flowers along the rim of the container and shorter flowers in the center.

The ideal flat-style arrangement will look attractive when viewed from any direction.

In practicing this style, it is important to bring out the strength or weakness of individual materials as well as the contrast between dense and more open areas.

꽃과 꽃의 간격이 같지 않게
꽃과 꽃의 높이가 같지 않게
바깥쪽 꽃이 높게 안쪽 꽃이 얕게, 꽂았을 때 安定感이 있다.

四方 어디서 보아도 빈 구석이 안보이는 잘 정리된 꽃은 아름답다.

각기 素材가 가지는 強弱 疎密의 度를 分明히 하는 것은 平面型 꽃을 꽂는 데 있어 重要한 일이다.

Materials: Rose, gentian and patrinia
Container: Onyx flower vase

素材 薔薇, 용담, 마타리
花器 오닉스花瓶

Materials:
Daffodil, anemone
and asparagus
myriocladus
Container: Iwata
glass container
素材　데포딜,
아네모네,
미리오그라다스
花器　유리花器 (岩田)

Materials: Tulip
and sweet pea
Container:
German container
with a handle
素材　튜울립,
스위트피－
花器　독일製
손잡이유리花器

Materials: Holly,
poinsettia and rose
Container: White
porcelain water basin
素材　호리,
포인세티아,　薔薇
花器　白磁水盤

Use of Aged Wood　古木의 構成

When using aged wood in flower arrangement, you should first be aware of the shape of the wood. Each piece of aged wood has unique characteristics in terms of weight, volume, strength, line and surface.

You can create harmony through well-conceived combinations of aged wood, containers and other materials.

古木의 構成에 있어 각기 古木의 形態나 質感을 잘 파악하는 일은 매우 重要한 課程이다.

古木은 나무에 따라 重量感, 强한 힘도 나타내 주지만 그 構成에 따라 輕快한 線의 움직임이나 空間構成으로 다른 느낌을 주는 多樣한 作品을 構成할 수 있다.

花器와 古木 그리고 다른 素材들이 一體가 되었을 때 作品이 完全하게 이루어진다.

Materials: Clematis, Japanese winterberry, and aged tree
Container: White porcelain bowl

素材　크리마티스, 落霜紅, 古木
花器　白磁鉢

Materials: Orchid and aged tree
Container: White porcelain water basin
素材　洋蘭，古木
花器　白磁水盤

Natural Arrangement-
Narcissus
自然의 生態에 忠實하게
(水仙花)

It is essential in flower arrangement to retain the natural characteristics of plants.

Narcissus is one example. As shown in the photo, the placement of narcissus flowers and the lengths of their of leaves can be freely decided by basing your choices upon the knowledge of naturally grwoing narcissus flowers, stems and leaves.

In this case, we remove the stem and leaves from the white base of the narcissus (Photos 1-3), rearrange four leaves and one stem, and reinsert them into the white base as if they were growing naturally that way (Photos 4-8).

素材가 지니고 있는 自然의 生態를 그대로 살려서 꽃을 꽂는 것은 重要한 일이다.

作例에서 보는 水仙花에 있어서 잎의 길이와 꽃의 앉음새를 마음대로 調節할 수 있는 것은 自然의 生態를 잘 알기 때문이다.

水仙花의 白根에서 꽃을 먼저 빼내고 안쪽 잎부터 꺼낸 다음 잎길이를 調節하여, 自然의 水仙花와 같은 狀態로 바깥 잎부터 白根 안에 넣고 마지막에 꽃줄기를 넣는다.

Materials: Narcissus and moth-convered plume
Container: Celadon porcelain vase
素材　水仙花, 이끼붙은 梅花나무
花器　青磁花瓶 (申相浩)

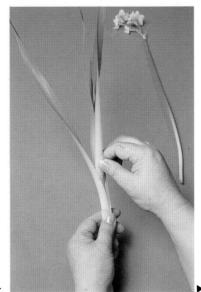

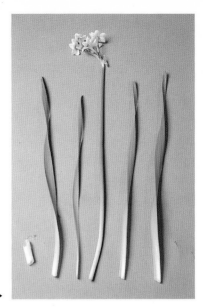

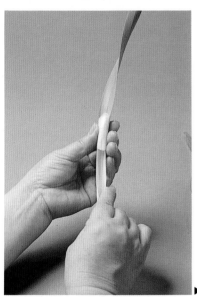

White base of narcissus
Reinser leaves into white base.

水仙花　白根

Front view
正面

Side view
側面

Back
後

Front
前

White base　白根

Flowing stem　花

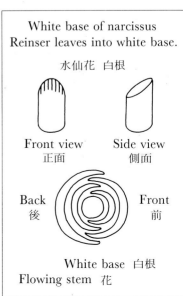

White Porcelain Vases

Yi Dynasty white porcelain ware is one of the many types of ceramics made in Korea. Along with celadon porcelain ware from the Koryo era, white porcelain ware is highly valued worldwide.

The Yi Dynasty white porcelain containers we sometimes come across today were originally created for casual use, with the techniques common to the period. Yet although our modern porcelain techniques are far superior, I cannot think of another type of pottery that gives a greater sense of stability and conveys the beauty of flowers better than (Yi Dynasty) white porcelain containers.

These containers are magnificent and powerful, imbued with a vitality which is strongly appealing. Even the larger ones have a sense of lightness about them; with their greater mass they project a feeling of softness and warmth, making it hard to imagine that they are porcelain, burned at temperatures that goes up as high as 1400 degrees centigrade. The smaller containers don't seem shrunken or compressed—they present a serene picture of refined grace.

All Yi Dynasty containers are somewhat mysterious. The smooth, unvarying surface of each Yi Dynasty white porcelain container creates an image of a calm and composed world, ready for any eventuality.

The contours of white porcelain containers are simple and strong, and seem to extend infinitely, as if promising immortal life. If you look closely from various perspectives, you find that the white color of the porcelain actually combines hundreds of different hues.

More than thirty years have passed since I became fascinated by the beauty of combining white porcelain containers and flower arrangement.

While being sources of pleasure by themselves, the white porcelain vases have also provided me with incentives for exploring further the world of flowers.

I came to want to create vases of my own, more suited to the needs of daily life and modern living environments. I wanted to achieve this by using the techniques and aesthetics of past days. These vases of my own design would increase my enjoyment and appreciation of flower arrangement.

In 1974 I built a kiln in Wha Kong Woun, where it is known that kilns existed as far back as a thousand years ago. In fact, the original name of the village was Bookokri, meaning the village of the kilns. In my kiln, I recreated the exact process of producing white porcelain used in the Yi Dynasty, including burning entire pine trees. While I work, I gather fragments of the porcelains made by our ancestors and try to imagine their lives... this provides moments of relief from modern-day pressures.

From every step of the whole long process to produce white porcelain ware, I sense that fire, clay and people have become one, with the final say of God, the process culminates in a finished work of art. For me, nothing can compare to the joy and splendor of matching flowers with these powerful white porcelain vases.

白磁와 나

李朝白磁는 韓國의 陶磁器 중에서 高麗時代의 青磁와 더불어 세계에 자랑하는 磁器다.

때때로 만나는 白磁는 옛날 사람들의 環境에서 必要에 따라 당시의 技法으로 만들어진 것인데 지금의 꽃을 꽂는 나에게 있어 白磁만큼 꽃을 아름답고 더욱 安定感을 가져다 주는 그릇은 따로 찾을 수 없다.

그릇이 커도 무겁게 보이지 아니하고 부푼 속에 잠겨있는 圓滿함은 千四百度의 高熱로 구워낸 磁器라고 생각지 못하도록 부드러움과 따뜻함을 느끼게 한다.

形態가 작은 李朝白磁라도 그것들은 옹졸하지 않고 의젓한 氣品을 갖추어, 너그러운 모습은 작으면서도 大人의 風采가 엿보이는 정말 신비한 그릇이다.

李朝白磁의 살결은 반짝이지 않고 뽐내지 않고 침착하며 무엇이든지 받아들이는 寬容을 느끼게 한다.

白磁의 線은 單純하고 힘차서 무한히 뻗어가는 永遠한 生命을 지니고 있어 한가지 白色이 백가지色으로도, 천가지色으로도 느껴지게 한다.

李朝白磁와 꽃과의 만남에 끌리어서 三十餘年이 흘러갔다.

옛날 사람들이 만든 그릇이 아닌, 지금 우리들의 生活에 必要한 그릇, 지금의 生活空間에 꽂을 수 있는 그릇을 옛날 사람들의 白磁의 感覺과 技術을 導入하여 나 自身의 그릇을 만들 수 있는 길이 열렸다.

1974年 華公苑 안에 白磁를 굽는 용가마를 만들었다. 소나무를 때고 全 工程을 옛날 사람들과 같은 技術로 進行시키는 가마다.

이상하게도, 華公苑은 千年前에 가마가 있던 곳으로 고을 이름도 釜谷里 또 가마골이라 한다.

선인들이 남겨 놓은 磁器조각을 주우면서 생각이 千年前으로 거슬러 올라갈 때가 忙中閑의 時間이라고나 할까.

흙과 불과 사람이 一體가 되어, 神만이 絶對의 힘으로 創造하는 이 일은 긴 과정의 하나하나가 最後의 作品으로 結晶된다.

神秘하게 숨쉬는 白磁를, 꽃과 같이 하는 때의 기쁨과 황홀함을 무엇에 비할 수 있으랴.

Brief Personal History of Im Wha Kong

Im Wha Kong was born in 1924 in Kang Won Do, Korea, where her grandfather had established the family home. Her grandfather gave Wha Kong her name and was a great influence on her in many ways. A strong advocate of traditional Korean arts and culture, he also cultivated flowers with tender loving care. If his flowers bloomed to his satisfaction, he would invite guests to his home.

After graduating Kyeon-gi Public Senior High School for Girls, Wha Kong was given the chance to study under a Japanese ikebana (flower arrangement) teacher living in Seoul. Her two years of study were also very influential in directing her towards a "life with flowers."

In October 1958, the first small Floral Art Exhibition was sponsored by the United States Information Service (USIS). About the same time, Nyeo Woen, the publisher of a woman's monthly magazine, began to conduct flower arrangement classes on a regular basis with Im Wha Kong as an instructor. This attracted the attention of mass media, which opened the era of post-war Korean flower arrangement.

In 1960, flower devotees, both in Korea and abroad, who had studied with Im Wha Kong, established the Im Wha Kong Flower Arrangement Society. The members first exhibition, organized by Im Wha Kong, was held in 1960. In 1973, the group was organized as the Wha Kong Hoe Corporation. In April 1990, the 54th Wha Kong Hoe Exhibition was held at the Westin Chosun Hotel.

In addition to holding exhibition in Korea for more than 30 years without a break, Mrs. Im has held many exhibitions and demonstrations all over the world, including Japan, the U.S. and Asian countries. Everywhere she has gone, she has cultivated warm friendships with other lovers of flowers.

In a 1980 tour of North America, the Garden Club of Washington D.C. organized an exhibition for her. She also gave demonstrations in Seattle and New York, using very different floral materials. In New York, she was overwhelmed when presented with a rare and magnificent bonsai tree to use in her arrangement.

In October 1981, in Lima, Peru, a museum was used as the exhibition hall. The exhibition and accompanying reception, featuring a military band, were attended by the President's wife.

Mrs. Im has participated four times the Philadelphia Flower Show in the U.S. since March 1984, and each time has been an opportunity to strengthen friendships and understanding. During the latest visit, she was delighted to be asked to give a demonstration from the Longwood Garden.

In April 1985, Im Wha Kong received an invitation from the Chancellor of Smith College in the U.S. Since she had wanted to go there since childhood, this visit held special meaning for her. After demonstrating flower arrangements, Mrs. Im stayed at the Chancellor's Official Residence. The dreamlike sight that greeted her when she awoke during her stay, of small boats floating on a nearby pond, became a special memory.

In November 1985, Mrs. Im was invited to the Netherlands. A museum built on a canal bank, the Official Residence of the Korean Ambassador and the Municipal Government Office were all used as her exhibition halls.

In April 1988, she gave a demonstration at the Tangerine Club in Singapore. The special stage featured Korean furniture and her originally designed white porcelain containers.

In May 1989, the rows of hose chestnut trees near the marquee at the Chelsea Flower Show in London with their masses of pink blossoms, presented a memorable sight. However, Im Wha Kong will never forget the pink herbaceous peonies and the iris leaves she was allowed to cut for the show from the famous garden.

In November 1989, Mrs. Im was awarded the 30th Anniversary Commemorative Cup by Ewhr Women's University of Home Economics and Social Sciences, where she had been a lecturer since 1959.

Today, the Wha Kong Hoe Corporation Hall near the Museum of Seoul is a place of study, training and community for all of it members and the many friends of flowers from around the world.

1924年, 祖父의 代에 落鄕해 있던 江原道平康에서 出生.

華公이라는 이름은 今日의 그를 豫知하셨던가 祖父께서 지어 주셨다. 祖父께서는 李朝人의 生活樣式을 固守하셨다.

京畿公立高等女學校 卒業後, 서울에 살던 日本 生花教授에게 師事할 機會가 있었다.

二年餘의 修業은 짧은 期間이었지만 祖父와 더불어, 후일 그의 꽃生活에 큰 影響을 미쳤다.

1958年 10月 第一回 華藝小品展이 美國公報院(U.S.I.S.)에서 열리고 같은 時期에 女性月刊誌 女苑社가 定期華藝講習會를 始作했다. 이것을 계기로 하여 新聞 雜誌 및 放送도 呼應하여 戰後 韓國 華藝의 幕이 열렸다.

꽃으로 맺어진 內外의 會員은 1960年 任華公꽃꽂이同友會를 設立하고 1973年에 社團法人 華公會로 改編하였다.

1960年에 第一回 華公會 主催 會員展을 始作으로 年二回의 展示會를 거듭하여 1990年 4月 第五十四回 華公會 會員展을 웨스틴 조선호텔에서 開催하였다.

三十餘年間 끊임없이 國內의 會員展을 가진 外에 東京, 北美, 南美, 유-럽, 아시아의 여러 나라에서 많은 展示會와 데몬스트레이션을 가졌다.

워싱턴 D.C.의 展示會와 데몬스트레이션은 1980年 가-든클럽 主催였다.

뉴욕 시애틀에서는 각기 꽃을 調達하는 過程은 달랐지만, 훌륭하게 기른 庭園木을 잘라 素材로 썼을 때는 송구함과 따뜻한 꽃친구의 友情을 피부로 느끼며 꽃을 꽂았다.

페루 리마에서는 博物館을 展示會場으로 使用했는데 大統領夫人의 入場과 同時에 演奏되는 軍樂隊의 音樂속에서 리셉션이 시작되었다. 1981年10月.

1984年 3月부터 5回에 걸쳐 參加한 美國 필라델피아 플라워쇼-에서는 친구도 많이 사귀고 主催側하고도 理解가 깊어져 오랜 벗같이 되었다. 有名한 롱-우드가-든의 아름다운 꽃과 古家에서 이루어진 데몬스트레이션도 印象깊었다.

少女時節 憧憬하였던 美國 스미스 칼리지 學長으로부터 招請받아 華藝 데몬스트레이션을 마치고, 學長公舘에서 묵은 이튿날 아침, 창 너머로 본 꿈같이 아름다운 연못에 떠 있던 작은배를 平生 못잊을 것이다. 1985年 4 月.

네델란드에 招請되었을 때의 데몬스트레이션 會場은 運河기슭에 있는 博物舘과 韓國大使舘邸 및 市廳이었다. 1985年 11月.

1988年 4 月에는 싱가폴의 歷史가 깃든 탱그린클럽 스테이지에 한국 古家具와 白磁로 채워진 속에서 示範이 이루어졌다.

런던의 체시플라워쇼ー의 텐트밖에 줄섰던 핑크色 마로니에꽃은 쇼ー가 끝날무렵에 졌다. 이 쇼ー를 위해 위슬리 가ー든에서 꺾게 해 준 창포잎과 빨강색 芍藥꽃 등을 잊을 수가 없다. 1989年 5 月.

1979年 華藝 I, 1984年 華藝 II, 1983年 華藝 百人輯 I, 1987年 華藝百人輯 II가 出版되었다. 主婦의 友社에서.

1989年 11月에 1959年부터 出講한 梨花女子大學校 家政科學大學으로부터 30週年 感謝牌를 받았다.

現在 서울中央博物舘 가까이에 있는 華公會舘은 널리 世界의 꽃친구들과 會員들의 研修와 親善의 자리가 되고 있다.